DON'T FORGET TO PARENT

By

Chioma Imo

Published by:

Chioma House Publishing

1322 Space Park Dr, STE A211 Bldg A

Houston, TX 77058 United States

Printed in the United States of America

DEDICATION

To every parent doing their best—

may you lead with love, clarity, and courage.

THANK YOU

Thank you, Erika, for encouraging me to write this book.

Thank you for helping with the outline of the book and for your unwavering support and friendship.

DON'T FORGET TO PARENT

When Parenting Gets Replaced by Friendship, and Kids Pay the Price

Introduction: The Moment I Started Seeing It Everywhere

As I get older and raise my son who is now 16, I notice things I used to overlook. Not because they weren't happening but because I didn't have eyes for them at the time. There's something about watching your own child grow that makes you pay attention to other families differently. You start listening to and hearing what families say at the grocery store. You start noticing how children respond or don't respond to adults. You start realizing that what looks "small" is often the beginning of something much bigger.

I see so many parents that try to be their children's friends. Why is this? Why do parents want to be their children's friends?

It's not that closeness is wrong. It's not that laughter is wrong. I have seen that there's a shift that happens when "friend" becomes the role and "parent" becomes optional. The issue I see when this arises is that the kids behave a certain way. They don't listen to authority because their authority figures did not teach them to listen to them. And so many parents will say, "they don't listen to me," or "you can't tell them what to do."

How does this happen? Why does this happen? I believe it happens because parents forget to parent.

This book is me putting into words what I've been watching and what I've learned while raising my son.

Chapter 1: The Psychology of Being Your Children's Friend

Vignette: The Conversation in The Parking Lot

It was a sunny ordinary afternoon that didn't feel important until later. I was in a parking lot at the grocery store, walking inside while watching people come and go, parents with kids, kids with attitudes, kids with headphones, kids with faces that said, "Don't talk to me." A mother walked closely behind me with her daughter. My guess was that the girl couldn't have been more than twelve or thirteen years of age.

The mother said something gently, something a parent would say, like "Come on, walk faster". Her daughter snapped, loud enough for strangers to hear, "Stop! You're doing too much." In that moment, I could only imagine that hard eye rolling and look of disdain she must have given her mother. It was like I could feel her eyes rolling and I was not even involved.

I waited curiously for her mother to respond. The mother seemed as if she did not know how or what to respond. What shocked me more than the child's tone was the mother's response. She immediately softened, almost like she was negotiating with a coworker and responded, “Okay, okay, I'm sorry… I just want you to walk faster is all”.

I remember thinking: Why did she feel the need to apologize to her daughter? What motivated her to do so? I was perplexed.

I recall another incident. I was at a high school track meet sitting in bleachers full of parents and onlookers. A dad was talking to his teenage daughter about something. As she was leaving him and walking down the bleachers a few feet away from him, he called her name to return to him. She turned to him, stretched out her arm, palm facing him and loudly said, “talk to the hand not the face, talk to the hand”, and turned around and continued to walk away. I was mortified at how she spoke to her dad. He just laughed it off and said, “kids”.

That's when it hit me. In both instances, this wasn't parenting. This was fear. Fear of not being a “friend” to their children. Fear of losing them. Fear of receiving further embarrassment from their child therefore it is easier to acquiesce. The path of least resistance.

The psychology of why you feel you need to be your children's friend is deeper than we like to admit. What is the psychology behind this phenomenon?

Sometimes it's guilt. You feel like you've been busy. You feel like you haven't done enough. You feel like you owe them. Sometimes it's loneliness. Sometimes a child becomes the emotional companion; someone you vent to, someone you “kick it” with, someone you rely on for comfort. Sometimes it's fear. This fear could make one feel that if you push too hard, your child might pull away and you'll lose them. If you push too hard, your child will shut down and not communicate with you.

But children don't need you to chase their approval. They need you to provide stability.

When parents choose friendship over authority, children learn something quietly but powerfully and that is that boundaries are optional. That “no” doesn't mean no. That the loudest feelings win. Gradually this leads kids to begin to behave a certain way. They don't listen to authority because their authority figures did not teach them to listen to them.

Then later, the same parent says, “they don't listen to me” or “you can't tell them what to do.” Or worse, “they have a mind of their own”. And I always want to ask, How does this happen? Why does this happen?

It happens when parenting becomes emotional bargaining.

Being loving is not the same as being led by your child's mood. It's okay for your child to be upset. It's okay for them to disagree. It is ok to say, “no”. But it is not okay for them to have a stronghold over their parents. This is not acceptable.

I say this as someone still learning, still growing, still watching myself. I believe it happens because parents forget to parent.

Chapter 2: The Biblical Component — Training, Discipline, and Love

Vignette: The Verse That Follows Me

There are biblical components to raising a child. There are verses I grew up hearing that you don't fully understand until life makes them real. For me, one of those phrases was: "train up a child in the way he should go and when they are old, they will not depart". When you really think about this verse, this means either raising them the right or the wrong way.

Whichever way a parent raises their kids is the way they will go. You choose.

The word "train" is a very interesting word. It can have both positive and negative connotations. Positively, the word "train" often symbolizes progress, efficiency and connectivity representing life's exciting journey that often bring people together. It is also about nurturing and guiding our children. It is about developing good virtues, values and knowledge. Negatively, the word, "train", can imply rigidity, stagnation, lack of personal growth, lack of good judgement, poor character, and disrespect. How we train our children is how they will go.

That word “train” is not soft. Training is consistent. Training is intentional. Training requires repetition and follow-through. Training means you don't change the rules just because your child is irritated. Furthermore, you don’t change the rules just because the truth might not set well with your kids.

Another verse reads: “whoever spares the rod, hates their children but the one who loves their children is careful to discipline them.” This word “rod” is a metaphor for discipline and guidance.

That matters because a lot of people misunderstand it. They assume discipline means harshness. But the verse says “careful.” That means discipline is thoughtful. It is guided. It is purposeful. It is not emotional revenge. It is love with structure.

I've seen parents who avoid discipline because they believe love means constant softness. But real love isn't afraid to correct.

What can happen if you don't train? Someone else will. Life will. Peers will. Culture will. And those teachers don't care if your child breaks.

Chapter 3: Mentoring, Principles, and the Question We Avoid

Vignette: The Adult Who Admitted They Still Needed Help

I had a conversation with a male friend of mine. This man is an adult, very successful President of a major corporation and highly respected. He said to me, "I need mentoring." He said it without shame. Like it was normal. Like it was wise.

And it made me pause because I thought: If he, an adult, President of a major corporation, can openly admit that he needed mentoring/guidance, why do we act like children don't?

If we adults need mentoring, why do we think our children don't need parenting? That question exposes something important.

We join programs. We hire coaches. We seek counseling. We ask for advice. We ask someone older and wiser, "Help me see what I don't see."

But then we look at children who are literally still developing, and we treat parenting like something optional. Like children should lead themselves. Like they should "just know."

This is why principles matter. Are you raising them on principles? Are you raising them on something steady? Something consistent? Something that does not shift with your emotions or your fatigue.

Because if you don't raise them on principles, they get raised on preferences. And preferences change. Moods change. Fear changes. Convenience changes.

A child who is raised on principles learns:

- what's right, what's wrong
- what your home stands for, what is expected
- what has consequences

And that's not controlling, it's grounding.

Mentoring is not a weakness. Parenting is mentoring with authority. Children need it even more than adults do.

Chapter 4: Boundaries, Accountability, and Why "No" Feels So Hard

Vignette: The Conversation Nobody Wants

There was a moment, a quiet, personal moment when I realized something about boundaries: they expose you.

If you think about it for a moment, the second you draw a line for your child, you must face whether you have crossed that line yourself.

And that's when parenting stops being a speech and becomes a mirror. You see because a lot of what our children learn is from what they see as compared to what we say.

Establishing boundaries and what's right and what's wrong is where many parents struggle the most. Why is it hard to tell our children no and why is it so hard to determine boundaries?

Is it because that means we would have to be held accountable? Sometimes, yes.

Is the reason we cannot tell our children not to drink or smoke because we are drinking and smoking too? Or because then our kids might say to us, "well you are doing those things?" Do we just brush it off and say, "well we are adults and you're not." Or do we make it any better by allowing our kids to drink but only in our home? Only in our presence? What are we teaching them?

What are we saying to them? We are too busy trying to be the "cool" parent, their friend. So, I ask, what kind of examples are we showing them?

A child is watching how you justify. How you excuse. How you shift blame. How you set boundaries for them but not for yourself. Again, children learn mostly from what they see.

And then we wonder why they push back. Why they challenge. Why they don't accept correction from us. They learned the art of arguing from the adults who modeled it.

This is where the question, why would you do this and why is this acceptable, materializes.

So many behaviors become "acceptable" not because they're healthy but because we're tired. Or embarrassed. Or we don't want conflict. Or we don't want to explain ourselves.

Boundaries aren't cruelty. They're clarity. And clarity is safety.

Chapter 5: Lazy Parenting, Guidelines, Manners, and the Entitlement Mentality

Vignette: The "Thank You" That Never Came

When I was growing up, my parents taught me to say "thank you" to people that did things for me or that paid me a compliment, or that helped me with something. Not only did my parents verbally teach me to say thank you to others but they modeled it in our home. They said "thank you" to one another and to their children. "Thank you" was commonplace in our home. That set the tone of how to treat others. "Thank you" is missing a lot in kids today. It feels like it has been replaced by an entitlement mentality. I truly don't believe it is the fault of the kids. I believe it derives from lazy parenting.

Lazy parenting is not always dramatic. It can be quiet. It can be subtle. It can look like exhaustion. It can look like "I don't feel like dealing with it." It can look like letting small things slide until the small things become the culture of your home. Lazy parenting becomes a snowball effect.

Lazy parenting includes:

- Not setting guidelines
- Correction avoidance
- Picking comfort over discomfort

Whatever the reason for lazy parenting, we sweep things under the rug.

But when we sweep enough, your child learns, “They don't mean what they say.” Then manners disappear.

When manners disappear, you end up with kids not saying thank you to people when people do things for them. No appreciation. No gratitude. Is this something taught in the household by the lack of example shown?

Yes, often it is. Gratitude is learned by hearing it, seeing it, being corrected into it, and living inside a home where appreciation is expected.

When gratitude isn't trained, entitlement mentality grows. Entitlement mentality says:

- “I know I deserve this.”
- “I know people owe me.”
- “I don't have to appreciate anything someone does for me.”
- “Why wouldn’t they do it for me anyway”?

And this entitlement mentality doesn't just affect

mannerisms. It affects relationships, work ethics, respect of others, the ability to take corrections, and just a whole gamut of other things too numerous to mention.

Guidelines are not about nitpicking.

They're about preparing your child to live in a world that will not cater to them the way a parent might.

Please Don't Forget to Parent

In raising my son, I've learned that parenting is not about winning arguments. Parenting is about building responsible adults of good character. It is about loving your child enough to always correct them despite the potential fallout from them. It is about accepting that sometimes parenting can be uncomfortable.

Parents forget to parent when they try to avoid discomfort. When they want their children's approval more than they want their children's growth. When they confuse love with constant yes.

Love looks like:

- training, boundaries, correction
- discipline and guidance, principles
- guidelines, manners, gratitude

And yes, sometimes love looks like "no."

Because "train up a child…" isn't just a verse. It's a blueprint. And the "rod" as a metaphor for discipline and guidance is not about harm, it's about direction.

Don't forget to parent.

When parents forget to parent, children don't just lose rules, they lose direction.

NOTES

www.ingramcontent.com/pod-product-compliance
Lightning Source LLC
LaVergne TN
LVHW010946110826
845149LV00013B/2776

* 9 7 9 8 9 9 3 3 7 8 0 7 7 *